Poisonous Thoughts

Alex Johnson

Lafayette, Louisiana

Poisonous Thoughts
Copyright © 2020-21 Alex Johnson
Cover Art © 2020 Jessalyn Newton and Mike Bourque
Book and Cover Design © 2021 Alex Johnson and Jonathan Penton

All Rights Reserved

Fifteen Dollars US

ISBN 978-1-7356488-0-4

This project is supported in part by ArtSpark, an Individual Artist stipend supported by the Lafayette Economic Development Authority and administered by the Acadiana Center for the Arts. It was conceived, written, and planned in Lafayette, Louisiana as a Lyrically Inclined Production.

POISONOUS THOUGHTS

Alex Johnson

Contents

Letter to the Reader	9
Poison	11
Nigga I am	12
The Wolf	15
Close the Door	16
She Is I	19
Metaphysical Passion	21
Crown Black	23
Royalty	26
Letter to his new wife	27
New Iberia - January 30, 1889	29
Secrets	30
I Am Griselda Blanco	31
Void	33
Breaking News	34
Pure Is Your Touch	36
Power of Black Woman	38
Insecurities	40
Nouzout Creole	42
Acknowledgments	45
About the Author	46

for my teacher:
Your voice encourages me to keep going when I doubt my writing.
I am forever grateful for you Mrs. Fangue.

Dear Reader,

Thank you for choosing *Poisonous Thoughts* to add to your collection. It has truly been a journey creating this work. I chose *Poisonous Thoughts* as the title because it described my mental space. Poisonous, unhappy, unloved, worthless self-harming. I needed to heal. I needed to let go. I needed to write out the horde of thoughts clouding my ability to be happy. I share this experience with you to encourage you to stay in control of your thoughts. Do not let them overtake you. They do not define you. Your intention paired with action defines you. I use poetry as a tool to help me cope with my emotions. I encourage you to try it. It helps.

 Throughout this book you will find writing prompts with space to write. Please use them. They are designed to help you practice expressing your emotion through poetry. I hope you enjoy my special addition to my poetry book. Blessings to you and yours.

Alex

Poison

Where do you find yourself in your moments of silence?
Retracing every step
Imprinted into the ground
Call it "Cyclic Meditation"
Only to realize that she will never love you again
Closing doors right before you enter
Shut out
Out of lines tracing the past to erase the future.
What have you given her?
Blurred lines that mingle with your silhouette
Basking in your vanity
She would rather lose you than rattle the sanctity of her sanity
She could never be your Barbie Doll
Never dispose of her inner being to be led to broken promises
Covered by shards of her broken heart.
Separated
What have you become?
Finding your reflection in broken bottles that make room for your tears.
I often wonder what holds you here.
What binds you to this bottle
Captures your breath,
Holds you hostage…
Like submerging yourself in collected tears is not the same as attempted suicide.
It's time you came up for air

Nigga I am

Among all things he has come to be
in denial of the reflection of he
a slave to his own insecurities
restricted by his own boundaries
a paganish fool
separating the image of God
to accommodate mortal views.
Lost in sin
and divided at the core.
Rejecting the existence
of life's true lore.
The perfect picture of positivity
split into two.
Now negativity prevails
with flawless precision
severing the spirit from the root.
By law two negatives can never fuse,
leaving only the option for potential growth
or the chance to refuse
divine intervention
with an intention of a holistic method to heal.
Mind body and spirit turned against one
humanity left to the surreal.
Left to their demise
but despite the burning rope
he continues to hold his ties.
Walking around singing of
strange fruit hanging from the trees.
So caught up in life's melody
that he's forgotten to breathe.
Holding in all toxins.
Choking on severed pieces of his soul.
Purging positivity
so that pain can take control.
Lies bore holes through his teeth.
Flowing out tainting the earth
allowing deception to reside

where God's heart used to beat.
Rewording the definition of
how to be a man.
Sculpting man's image
with an unsteady hand.
Filling in the gaps with
platinum and gold.
Strutting around with a cheap swagger
swearing he's in control.
Spitting diamond encrusted lies
with a princess cut.
Screaming out to the heavens
"I just don't give a fuck! People will know me ocean to land! I more than a man, a Nigga I am!"

Writing Prompt

Learn to control your thoughts. If it is bothering you, write it out. What thought do you think of most? Create a metaphor that expresses what that thought feels like.

_____

_____

_____

_____

_____

_____

_____

_____

_____

_____

The Wolf

The wolf cried out
Late one night
He crept slowly to hide the light
Positioning his gaze

To believe it now
Would be so strange. Life will never be the same.
Yet, all these years he held her cold, a victim to his shame.
No longer could he only gaze

Upon her innocence
He longed to claim her scent
To peel the wrapping from her present
The fire in his eyes ablaze

She lay sleeping as he stroked her hair
Agitating his incontinence
Whispering to her beauty to aide his dominance
Sleep kept her in a daze

If her mother knew he would rue the day
He let his touch linger long
Coercing her to play along
He will burn in a blaze

Tonight the wolf cried out in grief
To his surprise she had a knife
Tucked beneath her pillow. Life,
His life, will soon part ways.

In anger she has lived too long,
Love had left her cold but strong.
Now, she doesn't have to play along.
The Wolf is finally gone.

Close The Door

Close the door
Walk in to the realm of the poor.
Where books can't describe
The measure of their strife
death is more appealing than the option of life.
No light around can brighten up the eyes of the youth.
When prosperity is a fable
and fear is the Truth.
No mercy
Only struggle written on their palms.
Fighting hierarchy
Spitting Bible verses quoted from Psalms.
Holding on to faith
While it rips at the seams.
Catching freedom
Barely by the tips of its wings.
Gasping for hope,
While the government blows smoke in their lungs.
Reassuring all that it's not just the Negros
That don't belong
and if you don't have the green
Then you will be taken by mainstream.
Stripped of all your worth left worthless
You won't even own the dirt beneath your knees.
Just decoration
Like a pedestal used to stack IOU's
You Owe Us
You Owe We.
Like property of the state
With declarations written in invisible ink.
Forget the word of man
You'll find more worth in the rust underneath your kitchen sink.
Like serving a side of blasphemy
With a main course of deceit is proper corporate etiquette.
And while they bask in all that's good
We can't even touch what's left of it.

And righteous has been castrated
and all that's left for them to do
is to elide and ostracize us.
While we fall to our knees
and beg for enlightenment.
Praying to be freed,
When we know the problem
but just won't let go of it.
And please realize that help is not on its way
and the only peace we can hope to attain
Is as a nation united.
Because as we are divided
We will never know more than pain

Writing Prompt

How far will you allow your self to drift? Imagine you are picked up by a gust of wind. Write a poem about your journey.

_____

_____

_____

_____

_____

_____

_____

_____

_____

She Is I
(The Red Queen)

She's lost herself in the inconsistencies
of her own mind.
Misinterpreting fabrications for reality.
Abusing her blessings
no longer humbled by her journey to true elevation.
Losing sight of how she'd come to fly.
Soaring through the solar
dancing amongst the stars.
Confusing dragons for angels
demons for lovers.
Not realizing that the world is a painting
not predefined by only black and white.
There are shades of gray
blues and greens
change is forever constant.
And life exists with or without
her or you or me or us.
Our existence precedes our understanding
but our purpose is as plain as the sun above.
Meaning that we are forever changing,
but here at each moment for a specific reason.
To penetrate the dark that envelops
the physical and metaphysical,
but her ignorance knows no bounds.
Limitless
infinite like the heavens above.
That same expanse that keep her
stationed amongst the ignorant.
Attached to pleasures of the flesh.
Tainting the purity of Love.
Believing that she is the definition of beauty
proud and strong.
Tangled in her own web of deception.
Blinded by her own greed, covetous.
Desiring to have everything not meant for her.

Claiming the entitlement of a queen,
but making false promises to her people.
Denying all knowledge, hopes and dreams that once crept from her lips.
And this false queen bears one name
as we commonly speak of her in reference to self.
She is I
but by our own vanity we cast her out of sight.
For her appearance is less than acceptable
in the eyes of perfect men.
Bound to the similarities between she and we
imperfections in a whole
stretching from limb to limb.
The coexistence of positive and negative can only go so far.
True realization and definition of self
must come from the eternal within
and be named as such.
For we all relate to this false queen
and should openly learn from her example of preservation of self
and ask ourselves
What is the difference between the queen and I?

Metaphysical Passion

I take interest in the divinities of your mind
wishing that I could be trapped inside
enslaved by time
never to leave the depths of you.
Caressing your most intimate features
metaphysical love
like floating amongst the clouds
with the wind moving slowly across you skin.
Like soft kisses from beyond my touch
kisses that leave you in a daze.
Lost in my passion
my beautiful slave.
My love is impalpable
no need for physical contact.
I'll have you trembling from your soul
to the small of your back.
Loving you internally without hesitation.
Every moment I spend within
brings out the ultimate sensation.
Taking every extra step to induce a natural high.
I'll have you to caught up in your senses to realize that I
have yet to lay a finger in you.
I've only been making love to your mind.
Taking your mind and body to places
unable to be seen with the mortal eye.
Teasing your soul with solemn I love yous
and a promise of a whole-hearted state of mind.
Incorporating divine Truth
with every simple slip of the tongue.
Granting pure pleasure
meant to compare distinctly to a seat beneath the sun.
Loving you eternally in ways the cause a pleasureful
sensation in that erotic place between your thighs.
You know those delightful occurrences
that spark a bright twinkle in a lovers eye.
Holding you close to ensure a spiritual connected state of mind.

Never thought a love could exist that would lead me to believe that humans could fly.
If only I could be trapped inside your passion
for days at a time,
There'd be no point in worrying about the physical separation between you and I.
Therefore,
the question of missing you is irrelevant.

Crown Black

How many times we gotta tell you we need you?

That you are worth more than crimson puddles in our streets,
That gunshots were not meant to swallow your heartbeat.
These broken mirrors have distorted your reflection,
but there are no more shackles on your feet.

Black Man

Your spirit resounds defeat.

Kush to LOUD,

VIBRANT in the streets.

Black Man Paranoia got you counting diamond bezels on your wrist,
Caressing Beretta triggers with your fingertips.
Cocaine white.
While you're still wondering why you family life is so distant.

Black Man

Don't you think we are tired of peeling your body from the pavement?
Explaining to your children why Daddy just can't make it,
Why Daddy just won't claim them.

If only we could inject our spirits into your hearts,
That way you would know you worth before the conversation even starts,

Black Man

We are tired of reminding you of the reasons you should love yourself.

God created you a King.

Black Man

Why don't you love yourself?

There is nothing else that the World can do for you,

Black Man
You gotta save your self,
Stop feeling sorry for yourself
Stop making excuses for your self
King. Please. Love yourself

Black Man

Are you listening?

Then why won't you put on your Crown?

Writing Prompt

Write it out. Whatever it is, don't let it fester. Write it out. This is a free write excercise, there are no instructions. You are in control. Write.

_____

_____

_____

_____

_____

_____

_____

_____

_____

Royalty

Imagine God gave you a crown,
Thorned and Tilted
Piercing like God left a card on the table that said,
"Those aren't diamonds my child. I pimped out your angels
be-dazzler. P.S. We love you."

Imagine it weighed all of God's transgressions,
His hopefulness
His love

Imagine the weight God felt when she learned,
That unlike Love, infinity does not come with conditions
It comes with purpose.
To teach that it is better to love fluidly, than to spend eternity
analyzing why it is so difficult for anyone to choose you.

To be creator of all that is and still told you aren't good enough.

Would you wear God's crown?
Or would you throw it away like the black, rainbow, vomit-colored
sweater my mom gave me for Christmas one year.

Would you cherish it?

Would you sign an agreement with humanity that says, "I will love
you despite your imperfections, even though I already know most
of you will leave me.
Will shun me when I need you most.
Mock my creations like prayer only translates to your voice.
That I vow to hold my regrets in silence, because vanity dripped
into your design the day I shed tears over sacrificing my son for
you."

Would you cherish God's crown?
Trade it for your own to relieve our Creator of her heartbreak,
Of his loneliness,
Would you spend eternity treating God like Royalty.

Letter to his new wife
For Katrina Broussard

How does it feel to know,
That your husband is a dead beat?
That he left your chambers late each night, creeping between her sheets...
And you...
Lying there...
Imagining their fingers interlocked,
Cringing at the thought of their embrace.
Pounding away at your foundation.
How many times did you question the fragrance of his malicious intent?
wafting past your nostrils,
the scent of roses on his fists.
Remnants of love blended with maroon silk pillowcases will not cleanse the essence of your malcontent, for his long deep kisses pressed against your lips.
Vile
Putrid
Disgusting
If only you knew how her youth,
Meant more to him then all he's left you with.
Yet memory of bruised kisses still linger at the edges of your smile
But at least you had enough money to hide your broken teeth
You labeled him a King bc he gave your ass my ring.
How long did it take you to realize the depth of his shallow intent?
7in, 8in, 9in, or did he just ask you to put the head in.
Yeah you can call me a bitch but Truth is, your desperation to have a man lead your spirit to beat to someone else's drum.
He left your bedding stained with your remorse,
His scent lingering,
Hovering
Did no one teach you the value of your smile?
That love is not meant to be like rubies dripping from your crown.

Queen, I pray you have the courage to get up.
Do not let his spirit weary your soul with reasons of why you
should not have voice
Let no weapon formed against you tame the essence of your spine
Even with his hands around your neck
Do not let him make you believe that you are worthless
You are not worthless...
Queen,
Please, stand up
fix your crown
And fight back

New Iberia - January 30, 1889
Response to 'The Lynchers'

You want me to not hate you
Scream yo name like da villan you are
Watch you grab my brother by his neck
Make red sea of his vessel
Drown him in white hatred
Like dem Louisiana canals don't run through his heart
Sha, dat bayou gon carry him to freedom no matter how much ya'll people do.
Dat water know the flavor of our kin
400 years of them tryna baptize their way to heaven
drowning Black skin
My people
got rage embedded in they ancestry
Dem white folk don't know no pain
Like laughter of coward on horse
Say that shit to our faces
Call us nigger again
Make it loud as knee against neck
Make him hold his breathe
Noose taught against windpipe

Just remember that,

WE ARE NOT AFRAID OF YOU

Secrets

When pain turns predator
World looks for reason to excuse his action
saving face means more than Truth

I Am Griselda Blanco
For Michael Corleone Blanco. R.I.P. Griselda Blanco

They call me La Madrina
The black widow
Say I baddest bitch in the land
I tell them I'm not Bitch
I'm a Lion, la leona
People cower at the sound of my voice
make everything my way
say I Godmother of cocaine,
Me, Griselda Blanco
La Reina Colombiana
I say, "I Entrepreneur, business woman."
If it weren't for me Pablo never would have made enough money to
build those hospitals,
but they call us criminals.
Well, maybe I did have a few bodies dangling from my web
Te mato por nada
but I'm no criminal
I'm a survivor
Since I left my mother's womb
God made me a fighter
una guerrera

11 years old he held me down
stroke my hair
mama tell me to pretend I like it
I am no one's puta
so I left my innocence in the bullet I put through his back
where was la policia when he taught my soul to capture innocent life
but they call me a monster
Why didn't any one come to save me?
When I had nothing
una nina
No one came to save me
Only God Kept me
Solo Dios me proteje

El que reza y peca, empata
"He who sins, but prays, breaks even."

I learned those streets with my head up
make passports so real
Even FBI no tell difference
there is nothing impossible for me
and at least I raised my boys to be men
Tell me I'm horrible mother!
i gave my children the life you dream of
the only way i knew to raise my sons! I did it!
I made them men. Strong.
Taught them to love each other
No one comes before La Familia.
Keep each other in prayer
in spirit
in love
mis amores
Maybe we no perfect like you
But we stand up for each other
for what is right
por la familia
I am proud of my sons
and I love them!
More than my parents could ever have loved me.
Yo, Griselda Blanco
am no monster
I am a survivor
a child de Dios
A warrior
I overcame
y I don't give a fuck what you think of me.

I am Griselda Blanco

Void

There is nothing here
    I search for understanding
    Answers escape me.

Breaking News

Our country has fallen to shambles.
Spread across the land like pieces of broken glass
being scooped up by politicians whose main interest is not to
compose a logical thought,
but to ensure that the fill of their wallets matches the color of their
lawn.
While the rest of us work through struggle,
Protest about struggle
barely livable conditions
The scent of magnolias fragrant in the air
people strugglin'
begging for our lives to matter,

I'm not angry, just concerned.

Blame can no longer only be placed on the elected
We have become a lot of drones
we've torn from the womb
and thrown into a system
we're molded to fit and live with in the popular consensus
created by false gods and corrupted idols
***Breaking News: Donald Trump has just confirmed that America is in
for a very serious problem***
created by false gods and corrupted idols
stripping all tools needed to build individuality
still we run blind through the world in search of guidance and
answers
avoiding all attempts to save ourselves
prayer, education, empathy
living a lie
dying without reason
fighting without purpose
our people strugglin'
we've lost the drive to save ourselves

I'm not angry, just concerned.
Progressing to our own destruction

blood spilled
sweat shed
lives given to ensure our freedom
and we throw it away for a dollar and a popular fad
This just in, the hover boards that do not really hover bc they have wheels are randomly catching fire.
Selling our souls to the highest bidder
Who are we and what do we stand for?
It only takes 1 to spread ignorance throughout generations.

I'm not angry, just concerned.

We are tainted by greed and materialism
diving into the abyss
with locks and chains
our people are crying for more than just freedom
more like mental stability
coping skills
instead we let go of the power
held within our hands
we are foolish
if you wanna call me that simple angry black female poet after this then that's just fine
bc our government shut down a long time ago and our people just won't get mad enough
How can we expect a government to represent us when we can't represent ourselves?
carried away with foolish things
trending down our twitter feeds
never understanding the True meaning of revolution.
We lack action
We lack empathy
We lack original

Distracted by screens that only tell of our demise.
We've lost sight of our purpose.

I'm not angry, I am just concerned.

Pure Is Your Touch

As days go by
I reminisce of your warm embrace
and the way I felt when my heart jumped to meet your finger tips.
Longing to rest in the palm of your hand,
while you engrave the profession of our love in its walls.
Etching the reflection of our passion
like the sun against the current.
You give my heart its rhythm,
my soul its reason,
my body its sensation.
Erotic and everlasting.
True to the senses
so pure is your touch.
No other could compare,
no one is enough.
And as you slowly out line the image of our love
piercing the flesh.
Allowing pure red passion to
stream down to your wrist;
drip down onto the earth.
Finding your place amongst God's creation
Giving life to all that is beautiful
making it truly perfect.
Like, like
the one song being played by my heart.
A melody you inscribed in each chamber
Playing it note, by note, by note
never missing a beat
and resonating like a djembe drum.
See I've never been so close to home.
So uplifted it couldn't be a natural high
and you must be heaven sent
at least a twinkle in God's eyes.
To have me suspended in the heavens.
No air, no planets, no limitations
a place where no love could be taken for granted

and in the palm of your hand
you hold all that is me.
Just a portrait and tale forever you and me.

Power of Black Woman

The day after Alton Sterling lost his right to breathe
Black Woman prayed to bury aggression

So they couldn't use emotion to justify suicide

Try to Lynch her dreams,

Say her screams ring too loud
When father lie bloody pavement_____
Tell her swallow anguish with opioids, Xanax
Prescribe her addiction

Say her torment sound too much like begging.
Like benefit
Body bent backwards

Tell her **HELP** smell too much like freedom
like dignity
Rather lodge her head under vehicle
Say rocks against naked flesh hurt less than bullwhip
than shot gun
That 10 minute cavity search is not rape
is justified
is only way to find source of Black Girl Magic

Tell media make her body
viral
Broadcast her pain
Like everyone is strong enough to take this
to adapt
Strong enough to survive
Then mock her trauma
When her womb aches of bullets declaring war against
water gun
Against illness
Against Infant
Tell her

no one care better for her children than system
than casket
Say her voice sound too strong, too loud, too vivid

Media ask her how she does it
How she continues
Most unprotected species on planet
All gladiator-spirit and faith

Black woman
tunnel beneath struggle
with prayer
Carry family through broken mirrors
So deception don't poison the seed

How much passion do they want black woman to bleed

She will never hide like fragile,
Officers forced to face their reflection

Fail to protect
Fail to serve

like black woman didn't nurse this nation strong
all red, white, blue

Lashes
on back
head up
because she knows freedom already
belongs to her
That no weapon formed against her shall prosper
There is nothing your can do to break her faith
Covered in the blood

Black woman already know,
that God gon' get you

How much passion do they need black woman to bleed?

Insecurities
for Dylan the Magic Man

There is no feeling in the world that compares to the feeling of being alone.
Confined to your own thoughts as their screams precede articulation.
Resonating pain to accent your flaws.
Drowning out your voice, securing those bars that hold you close.
They remind you
Remind you of every moment you dread.
They remind of you of
Well, you know
The bus stop
The lunch line
The classroom
Home
The mirror
More than anything
The mirror.
I know people say that every day is a new day,
But when I wake up,
Some things just won't go away.
So I stopped looking.
I thought if I didn't see me
Then they wouldn't see me
And all the pain would drift away,
But it didn't.
Naw
It didn't...
people always tell me that God doesn't make mistakes,
but that doesn't explain why I can't look at me.
Why
Every time I walk out my front door,
You remind me that I'm ugly.
why every time I stand,
You remind me that I am shaped funny.
why every time I raise my hand you ignore me
And every time I open my mouth to speak you remind me

That stupid is all I will be
why
Every time I look up at me,
There is nothing there.
Nothing.
Nothing but these translucent tears
Weighted by my imperfections
Hailing to cover up my footprints
I am nothing
Ive been nothing for so long that I have not learned my own voice.
I am nothing
But when,
When will you stop judging?
When will you stop criticizing?
When will you stop yelling?
And just stop
And love me.

Nouzot Creole
dedicated to St. Landry Parish, Louisiana

Find us in the heart of Creole – Cajun Country
Where we celebrate of freedoms in our native tongue
Our history preserved in oral traditions

Nouzot Creole

We gumbo of strength and love
Of grandma's sweet dough pies
And grandpa's wild stories of horses and trail rides
Of fights for freedom, for peace
Of okra worn hands, labored for protection
Of family, of friendship

Nouzot Creole

We people of St. Landry Parish
Where diversity and community is our strength
Our heritage woven from foremother's hands
Feel the beat of our celebration in the bellows of our zydeco
Groove to our 2-step
That French-African rhythm with Latin Charm and Cajun Flare

Ayyyee! Meh, tout kek chose!
Mon sha' come join us!
Where we make art of history and festivals of words

Nouzot Creole, Nouzot Acadien,
We family of many colors

Writing Prompt

Some poetry is aged in painful places. Describe what happens when your valve opens.

Acknowledgments

I am grateful for this pivotal moment in my life; the opportunity to publish my first book is a dream come true. *Poisonous Thoughts* has allowed me to journey through some of my darkest places with only my pen to cover me. It has nurtured me as I learn to tame my Scattered Thoughts. It has allowed me to see my future. I have grown.

    I want to thank Acadiana Center for the Arts and Lafayette Economic Development Association for their support throughout the ArtSpark Individual Artist stipend process. Thank you to Jonathan Penton and DM Media 337 for working with me through the production process of *Poisonous Thoughts*. Thanks to Patrice Melnick, Agnes Courville, Bishop John Milton, and Bruce Coen for their unconditional love and support. I want to thank my Creator for sustaining me. Thank you to my followers, readers and fellow poets for their encouragement to keep writing.

About the Author

Alex "PoeticSoul" Johnson is the founder and leader of the spoken word organization Lyrically Inclined, where she can be seen live monthly in Lafayette, Louisiana.

As a teaching artist, PoeticSoul works to expose children in rural areas to literary arts. She organizes the Community Stage of The Festival of Words in Grand Coteau, Louisiana and is a committee member for the Annual Festival of Words fundraiser, "Word Crawl."

She has worked as a teaching artist in the Lafayette Parish Juvenile Detention Home, where she empowered incarcerated youth to create a spoken word poem, "Eyes of the Sun." "Eyes of the Sun" was turned into two murals thanks to the sponsorship of the 24-Hour Citizen Project.

She has performed her poetry at numerous venues including the Nuyorican Café, Acadiana Center for the Arts, and Cité des Arts, for organizations like Englewood's You Got Served, 100,00 Poets for Change, Unlikely Stories, and the Blood Jet Poetry Series. She presented at the 2016 Split this Rock Poetry festival in Washington, DC and was featured as a 2017 Tedx presenter.

PoeticSoul was the recipient of the ABC Fund's 2018 ICON Rising Star Award and the Acadiana Profile 2019 Trailblazer Award. Her poetry has been featured in *The Southern View Magazine*. She has received her B.S. in Business Administration - Marketing at the University of Louisiana at Lafayette. Her album *Scattered Thoughts* can be found on iTunes, Google Play Store, Spotify, and Amazon.

For booking contact: PoeticSoul337@gmail.com

www.ingramcontent.com/pod-product-compliance
Lightning Source LLC
Chambersburg PA
CBHW031218090426
42736CB00009B/973